T0207598

Voices

A Collection of Poetries

Penelope Lynch Collings

AuthorHouse™
1663 Liberty Drive
Bloomington, IN 47403
www.authorhouse.com
Phone: 833-262-8899

Because of the dynamic nature of the Internet, any web addresses or links contained in
this book may have changed since publication and may no longer be valid. The views
expressed in this work are solely those of the author and do not necessarily reflect the views
of the publisher, and the publisher hereby disclaims any responsibility for them.

This book is printed on acid-free paper.

ISBN: 978-1-6655-6520-2 (sc)
ISBN: 978-1-6655-6658-2 (hc)
ISBN: 978-1-6655-6521-9 (e)

Print information available on the last page.

Published by AuthorHouse 08/25/2022

authorHOUSE

Contents

Dedication

I dedicate this book of poems to my Creator, my Lord and Savior. He has given me the wisdom, knowledge and confidence to write these poems. My mom, (Georgiana Lynch-Scott) my first teacher and role model. My husband (Ian) my partner in life, My son, (Samuel) my biggest cheerleader and supporter. Sarah Capers and Dr. Joyce Pilgrim my spiritual sisters and friends. My five siblings (Dawn, Lindon, Juliet, Loris and Lester) They all believed in me and taught me the truth about myself and the world.

I will continue to shine the light in the dark corners with love, patience and forgiveness.

Preface

This book of poems is called voices. It is for children, women, men and the elderly who have no voice. We are faced with many experiences in our lives. Some we can explain and others we cannot. I hope these poems will shed the light in the dark corners and bring us closer together in love and harmony with each other and our Heavenly Father.

Annamarie

Today is your day

We celebrate and honor you for all your great work in Education.

For me your name represents this:

A is for **adorable**, **amazing** woman.

    Who is always willing to help someone find an answer to a question.

N is for never giving up on others

N is for nourishing and caring.

A is for an all colorful and all purposeful in life.

M is for many amazing stories that you have shared about your struggles in life.

A is for an alright American, Italian Queen that shines in her own beauty.

R is for risk taking, resilient woman who has fought against all odds and still standing tall, healthy and ready to receive more abundant blessings.

I is for incredible, unbelievable, unstoppable woman, mother, friend, teacher and leader

E is for each and every day you'll find your self looking younger, feeling stronger because you have fought a good fight and are ready to move on to bigger and better dreams; you're on the move.

    "Ain't no stopping you now" you're really, really on the move.

By Penelope Lynch

Basic Education student of The Department of Education

B Brilliant students attending Mid-Manhattan Learning Center

A Assurance and confidence that you have in your self

S Someday very soon you will acquire your GED

I Interesting books that you must read at school and in your home

C Circumstances and obstacles that you must overcome to obtain your GED

E Energetic, encouraging teachers, counselors and administrators that will guide you each and everyday

D Don't give up just keep on aiming for the prize

U Understanding yourself and learning to understand the American government

C Climbing up to the top of the mountain and taking a good look at the universe

A Always looking forward and never backwards

T Teaching others as you travel along

I If you do not try you will never know what you could do

O Opportunity is knocking at your door. Open the door and walk through it.

N Now that you have made it you must help someone else to make it

    When you obtain knowledge talk it, walk it, eat it, sleep it and live it.

By Penelope Lynch

Beautiful Radiant Sunshine

Beautiful radiant sunshine way up yonder brightening the corner of Merrick Blvd!

Last week Saturday, the house across the street was on fire.

This week Saturday, there is a beautiful radiant sunshine way up yonder brightening the corner!

Oh, what a beautiful radiant sunshine way out yonder brightening the corner of Merrick Blvd!

Trees dying, leaves falling but there is a beautiful radiant sunshine way up yonder brightening the corner of Merrick Blvd.

Children of Apartheid

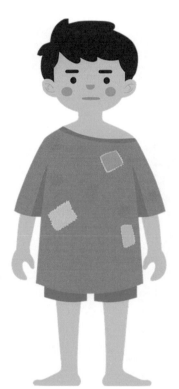

Why must the children suffer

Isn't it enough that you take away their Father?

Isn't it enough that there is no food to kill their hunger?

It is more than enough I say!

Just look at the numerous amounts who die everyday

What is worse than having no food to eat and no place to play?

You know what's worst?

I'll tell you what's worst!

What's worst is not having the medicine that young children need.

And do you not supply them with this just because of your own selfish greed.

Isn't it enough that you took away their right to enjoy their land?

Isn't it enough that they suffer through dehumanized system of Apartheid?

Not enough schools to go to and really learn.

Not enough food because their mothers rarely earn.

Not enough clothes to put on their backs.

One doctor for every 44,000 Africans and that's a fact.

Are you really proud of your color bar?

I have that feeling that the children will arise?

I have the feeling that these children will fight.

Suffer the children no more because one day these crimes you'll pay for!

By Penelope Lynch 1970

Come to the Big Apple

Come,

Come to the Big Apple

Come to the cold

The snow

The heat

The sun

Come to the Big Apple

Where in Winter there's a cry for Summer

And in Summer a cry is heard for Winter

Yes, come to the Big Apple

Come

Come see the brothers on 42nd Street

Falling but not falling

Flying high with holes in their arms

Under some triple X cinema

Yes, come to the Big Apple

Take a bite

Your first might be your last!

Come to the Big Apple

Come see the sisters playing ladies of the evening

Find love

Buy love

Sell love

There isn't anything you can't buy in the Big Apple

By Penelope Lynch 1974

Dear God,

Dear God,

On July 23, 2016 I had a conversation with my husband that was an eye opener. My sisters -in law and step children don't communicate with my husband and me because they feel that I have treated them very unfairly. As a Christian woman and a child of the King I apologize for my behavior and would love to have a harmonious family. Heavenly father please.

By Penelope Lynch – Collings

Dear Penelope,

God loves you and wants to make you the head and not the tail.

Your best days are ahead. "No weapon formed against you shall prosper."

He has an amazing plan for your life. He hasn't forgotten you.

He has created you for greatness.

Your name means patience, talented, creative, loving, purposeful, visionary, phenomenal woman.

God can use these qualities to make you great.

God counts you and sees you as a great treasure that he can use to do great things

You are a one of kind masterpiece, one of God's Jewels

You are qualified to do great things in 2019 and forward.

Great things will happen for you.

People don't determine your destiny.

God does.

God sees you as a beautiful woman that has outstanding marks to leave on this earth.

Think about the little boy with his five loaves of bread and two fishes, a miracle happened.

God chooses you today for greatness.

By Penelope Lynch

Do you know

Do you know?

Do you know?

Do you Know?

Oh!

Do you know who never gives up her seat on the bus.

She went to jail and spent the night in the doghouse, yes!!

She started the bus boycott which led to the Civil Rights movement.

Do you know Rosa Parks?

Do you know who is the man is on the one-dollar bill?

He was the man with the wood choppers, chop chop Ya 'll

Do you know George Washington?

Do you know who set the slaves free?

Took us away from captivity?

Old Abe was the man that set us free

Abraham Lincoln was there for you and me.

Do you know the man who had a dream?

That black and white children would live in peace and harmony.

He was assassinated but his dream never died.

Do you know Martin Luther King Jr?

Do you know who was the conductor of the Underground Railroad?

She had a price tag on her head.

She held a gun in one hand and the Bible in the other.

She was the biggest mother to the children of slavery.

Do you know Harriet Tubman?

Do you know the man who spent most of his life in jail on Robbin's Island and became the President of South Africa?

Do you know a man called Nelson Mandela?

Do you Know?

Do you Know?

Your history

There is still time for you and me.

Do you know?

Do you know?

Do you know?

By Penelope Lynch

Excuses

You said you used us because we were the only ones who could toil under the murderous sun of your soil . Then you said we loved it . We danced and gave praises to you for it, yes, so you said .You said it was the only way you were preaching God to us while you marked our backs with your words of the Lord .You said, we enjoyed being slaves because we never rebelled nor did one hand we raise. Yes, so you said. You said we were niggers, we could never be nothing but property, a nigger Nothing but your boy. Yes, So you said.

I don't want to hear no more, No more of your excuses for your rape and the scars that I bear. You were not capable of working on the plantation yet still you raped my nation . You said we danced and had fun. You never explained how you separated Mothers from their daughters and sons. You never said why we ran away . How we poisoned your food and even served threats to your life everyday.

This you never will say.

You never mention freedom fighters:

Like Nat Turner inspired by David Walker, who died for his "Appeal" No, you'll never teach us about Frederick Douglass or Harriet Tubman,

Yes, Our Black Moses . She always will be in the hearts of us the Black men and woman.

Never be nothing! Yet we invented and invented Do you know about the steam engine a black man invented? .We know now of Howard Latimer, Grandville T. Woods, Garrett A. Morgan, Jan Matzeliger, George Washington Carver. No, you'll never tell us what the Black man invented.

What? You fought the Civil War to free us.

You say lies. Lies! Just lies!

I know why you fought. It's not for the reasons why you taught.

You fought to keep your unions. Not because you thought of us as humans.

Lies! Lies!

Excuses, That's all you tell us.

Now we know the truth and the truth is what we'll teach the youth.

By Penelope Lynch

Faith

Faith is to believe
And when we believe
We will see the results
Of what we believe
It is only through faith
That we can reach Heaven.

By Penelope Lynch-Collings

Find Your Maker

Friend please find your maker.

For, we are living in perilous times.

Prayers are taken out of schools.

Mankind is building nuclear weapons to destroy each other.

Drugs and guns are easily acquired.

The government has legalized witchcraft.

There are so many churches in the world;

Some preaching Black power, some preaching White power and only a few preaching about the Power of our Almighty Father

I say again friends we are living in perilous times.

Please find your maker.

By Penelope Lynch 1973

Friend

Jesus Christ is the best friend that you and I could have.

He loves us during the bad times and through the good times.

He will never leave you.

He is always there whenever you need a friend.

God sent his only begotten son, Jesus Christ to teach us how to live.

He is the only friend that we should pattern our lives from.

We should not only call upon Him through the

bad times but we should call upon Him every day.

For without Him we are nothing!

Jesus Christ is the best friend that you and I could ever have!

Friend

Dear friend,

How are you? I just had to send a note to tell you how much I care about you. I saw you yesterday as you were talking with your friend. I waited all day hoping you would want to talk with me too.

I gave you a sunset to begin your day and a cool breeze to rest your head and I waited.

You never came by to say hello. It hurt me but I still love you because I am your friend.

I saw you sleeping last night and longed to touch your brow, so I spilled moonlight upon your face.

Again, I waited wanted to rush down so we could talk. I have so many gifts for you. You awoke and rushed off to work. My tears were in the rain.

If you would only listen to me. I love you. I try to tell you in the blue skies and in the quiet green grass. I whispered in the leaves on the trees and breathe in the flowers in the mountain streams, give the birds

Love song to sing. I clothe you with warm sunshine and perfume the air with nature scents.

My love for you is deeper than the ocean and bigger than the biggest need in your heart.

Ask me! Talk with me!

Please do not forget me. I have so much to share with you. I won't hassle you any further. It is your decision.

I have chosen you I will wait

I love you .

Your friend Jesus.

By Penelope Lynch

Glorious Day

Oh, what a glorious day to walk and talk about my Savior!

He has healed me from a cold and restored me back to health.

Oh, what a glorious Savior!

Sometimes we are so busy complaining about our challenges that we forget what He has done for us each and every day.

Lord, help me to remember each and everyday what you are doing in my life.

Lord, help me to remember to pray and worship you each and every day.

Oh, what a glorious Savior who loves us when we didn't love ourselves.

Oh, what a glorious Savior!

By Penelope Lynch – Collings

God is Love

God is love

We should love Him, because He first loved us.

Loving Him is keeping his commandments.

And not a burden we'll bear.

Nor a sorrow we'll share.

Our reward will be here.

Our hearts will be filled with care.

We will give our love to each one right here.

Salvation will be near.

For our Heavenly Father will be there.

By Penelope Lynch-Collings

Hope

Despite Global pandemic, millions of people dying, crime rising, homelessness and racism

There is hope.

Despite food shortages, many teachers, principals, superintendents overworked, remote schooling, teachers and principals delivering computers to student's homes and made wellness calls there is hope.

Online curriculum flooding in. Teachers kept students engaged through remote concerts, special video messages, songs and performances, drive by celebrations, students and family support groups.

There is hope.

Teachers created pantries and prayed with families, colleagues and friends as they worried about loved ones whose hospitals beds, they could not visit. While dealing with their own personal grief.

There is hope.

Despite the upgrade in technology so teachers can use various modes to communicate with their students, parents and the community. There are still several students who did not received the academic help that they needed.

There is hope.

There is hope and we must keep hope alive and trust and do our part to make this world a better place.

Looking Back

When I stop to look back at the way that I've come through the valleys I've crossed and the victories I've won. I would never have made it however hard I tried without the strong help of the Heavenly Father.

Love

The greatest thing in the world is love

Love is caring

Love is sharing

Love is forgiving

Love is patience

Love is kindness

Love is sincerity

Most of all

God is love

Where love is God is

For he that dwelleth in love

Dwelleth in God

By Penelope Lynch 1975

Obedience

Obedience is hard

But we must make a start

Then God will give us a part

If we do not depart from following our heart.

By Penelope Lynch 1972

Rules for Today

Do nothing that you would not like to be doing when Jesus comes.

Go to no place where you would not like to be found when Jesus comes.

Say nothing that you would not like to be saying when Jesus comes.

By Penelope Lynch 1972

What are We Doing for God?

What are we doing for God?

Are we working?

Are we weeping?

Are we sleeping?

Or

Are we reaping?

What are we doing for God?

Have we asked ourselves this question lately?

If no! Why not!

What are we doing for God?

We should be ashamed to even ask ourselves such a question

When we know how much Jesus Christ has done for us!

Again, I say What are we doing for God?

Have we given all to God?

Have we really surrendered all to God?

If we didn't then why not?

I say again what are we doing for God

Have we put ourselves first and God last?

Again, I say what are we doing for God

By Penelope Lynch 2013

What Does Thanksgiving Mean?

What does Thanksgiving mean?

To some it means gobble till you wobble

To some it means shop till you drop

To some it means spending time with family and friends eating delicious meals

To some it means praising God and giving Him the glory

To some it means the American Indians were driven out of their land

and given to the Europeans settlers

So, what does Thanksgiving means to you?

Who is George Washington Carver?

No one even remembers George Washington Carver the slave.

A man so great,

And yet so humble.

A man who bought so much to the human race.

He was known as one of the greatest scientists that ever lived….

He invented peanuts.

He invented dye.

He invented cheese.

He invented medicine.

He invented milk.

He invented synthetic cotton.

And other useful commodities that were used during the great depression.

And yet no one talks about him.

I wonder why?

And if they do.

They infer that he was not black.

But what God has created no man could destroy.

And his works will continue to be felt most proudly among those from which he came.

The poor oppressed and hungry.

By Penelope Lynch 1970

World Needs Love

What our world needs is Love

But we could only give love

When we seek or first love

Prayers are taken out of our public schools

Our children are killed in our schools and in the streets because of gun violence

Mental illness is rampant in our homes, schools, workplace and throughout the world.

Homelessness is increasing in our subways, streets and throughout the world.

Tornadoes, hurricane, tsunami and wildfires are destroying our communities.

5.94 Million people died from COVID - 19 in 2020 and more are dying daily.

Our hospitals are filled with sick patients, our health care workers are over worked. Many of our children are living in rat infested housing. Some housing complexes have no running water and no heat during the winter season.

Many of our children are sexual abused and killed by strangers or gun violence.

Our elderly citizens are neglected and treated like second class citizens

Many of our police officers and citizens are killed on the streets by gun violence.

Some of our politicians are fighting for power and wealth instead of working to improve our communities.

Our world can only improve unless we get back to finding our first love.

He is Jesus Christ.

When we have a relationship with Him.

We can love our brothers and sisters as we love ourselves.

What our world needs is love for our brothers and sisters.

We are all one, red, yellow, black and white we are all one in God's eyes.

Printed in the United States
by Baker & Taylor Publisher Services